# SIMPLIFIED GUIDE ON

# INTERNAL FAMILY SYSTEM THERAPY

Navigating Inner Worlds For Healing And Transformation – Key Principles And Practical Techniques For Self-Integration And Lasting Personal Growth

## DR. ARIYA REYNA

# CONTENTS

# DISCLIAMER

This book is intended for informational purposes only and is not a substitute for professional medical advice, diagnosis, or treatment. The information provided in this book is based on the author's research and personal experiences and is not meant to replace the advice of healthcare professionals.

Readers are encouraged to consult with their healthcare providers before beginning any new exercise, wellness, or health program.

 The author and publisher of this book are not responsible for any specific health or allergy needs that may require medical supervision and are not liable for any damages or negative consequences from any treatment, action, application, or preparation, to any person reading or following the information in this book.

The content of this book is not intended to be a substitute for professional medical advice, diagnosis, or treatment. Always seek the advice of your physician or other qualified health provider with any questions you may have regarding a medical condition.

The author and publisher disclaim responsibility for any adverse effects that may result from the use or application of the information contained in this book.

References to specific products, services, or organizations do not imply endorsement or recommendation by the author or the publisher.

The inclusion of such references is for illustrative purposes only. Thank you for reading and respecting the terms outlined in this disclaimer.

# CHAPTER ONE

## An Overview Of The Internal Family Systems Therapy

Internal Family Systems Therapy (IFS) is a distinct and effective therapy technique that dives into the intricate dynamics of a person's thinking. IFS, which was developed in the 1980s by Dr. Richard Schwartz, holds that the mind is made up of several sub-personalities or "parts," each with its feelings, ideas, and duties. These portions frequently act autonomously and may occasionally clash, resulting in internal strife and psychological suffering.

The core idea of IFS is that each and every person possesses an innate quality called the "Self."" The Self is the core, or real essence, of a person, and is defined by traits such as curiosity, compassion, and tranquility. IFS therapy's purpose is to assist individuals in developing a harmonious relationship with their internal components by increasing communication and comprehension.

# IFS Theoretical Foundations

IFS is influenced by different psychological and spiritual traditions, including systemic family therapy, psychodynamics, and mindfulness practices. The notion of plurality of mind is one of the major theoretical cornerstones of IFS. This viewpoint holds that the mind is a system of interacting pieces, each with its perspective and function.

The model also includes the concepts of "burdened" and "exiled" portions. The emotional weight of traumatic experiences is carried by burdened components, which frequently result in protective systems manifesting as defense mechanisms or maladaptive behaviors. Exiled portions, on the other hand, are pieces of the self that have been suppressed or pushed away as a result of trauma, usually in an attempt to cope with difficult feelings.

The innovative notion that even the most extreme and troublesome aspects have great intentions is introduced by IFS. Individuals can seek to alter their connections with these components by recognizing and embracing the beneficial intent behind them, resulting in better internal harmony.

## IFS Fundamental Ideas

### 1. Parts that work:

The notion of "parts work" is central to IFS, and IFS therapists assist patients in discovering and comprehending their distinct parts. This entails recognizing and defining the many roles that these components perform in an individual's life. Some parts may operate as guardians, sheltering the person from harsh memories or feelings, while others may bear emotional weights from previous experiences.

Individuals learn to distinguish themselves from their components through a process known as "unbending," which allows them to obtain a better grasp of their thoughts and feelings. Individuals can engage with their components in a more aware and purposeful manner as a result of this division.

## 2. Self-Leadership:

The necessity of establishing a relationship with the Self, which is regarded as the natural leader of the internal system, is emphasized by IFS. Compassion, curiosity, and tranquility are characteristics of the Self. Individuals are helped by therapists to deepen their connection with the Self, allowing it to take control of the internal system.

When people function from the Self, they may approach their parts with compassion and non-judgment, creating an atmosphere in which even the most difficult parts can be transformed. The objective is to build an internally harmonious society in which the Self directs and encourages the many elements toward integration and balance.

## 3. Protectors and Exiles Transformed:

Protective parts frequently devise techniques to protect persons from emotional distress. These defensive systems, however, might become troublesome and contribute to internal strife.

IFS seeks to alter these protective aspects by recognizing their positive intent and assisting them in performing their responsibilities more healthily.

Similarly, IFS strives to repair exiled portions of the self by providing a safe environment for these suppressed components of the self to be recognized and integrated. This procedure entails treating exiles with compassion and resolving unmet needs related to prior traumas.

## Internal Family Systems And The Self

### 1. The Self as a Concept:

The Self in IFS is not to be confused with the ego's traditional concept of the self. Instead, it refers to an individual's basic essence, which is a wellspring of knowledge and compassion. Curiosity, patience, and acceptance are characteristics of the Self. It acts as the internal system's natural leader, capable of creating harmony among the many sections.

## 2. Healing and Self-Leadership:

The premise that healing happens when persons work from the Self is central to IFS. Individuals who are connected to the Self may approach their parts with understanding and non-judgment. This self-leadership is critical in changing the dynamics of the internal family, resulting in better integration and balance.

## 3. Developing a Relationship with Oneself:

IFS therapeutic practice frequently includes assisting clients in strengthening their relationship with the Self. Mindfulness and self-reflection are two disciplines that are included in this process. Individuals can face obstacles with more internal serenity and wisdom as they grow more attuned to the attributes of the Self.

## 4. Compassionate Witness as Self:

In IFS, the Self acts as a caring witness to the many elements of a human. This witnessing is nonjudgmental and welcoming, allowing even the most difficult and damaged portions to be acknowledged and transformed. The Self's position as a witness is critical in instilling safety and trust inside the internal system.

Finally, Internal Family Systems Therapy provides a comprehensive awareness of the complexities of the human psyche.

Individuals can engage on a path of internal healing and integration by investigating the diversity of mind, admitting and reforming protecting and exiled components, and building a deep connection with the Self.

Parts work, self-leadership, and the transformational process are essential principles within IFS that provide a complete framework for therapists and individuals seeking a holistic approach to psychological well-being.

# CHAPTER TWO

## Internal Family Systems (IFS) Components

Dr. Richard Schwartz created the Internal Family Systems (IFS) treatment method, which sees the mind as a collection of several sub-personalities or "parts."" The term "parts" in IFS refers to distinct, semi-autonomous facets of an individual's personality that have different roles, perspectives, and emotions. Understanding and interacting with these sections, which might be protective or damaged, is an important feature of the IFS paradigm.

## Parts To Understand:

According to IFS, each individual has a core or genuine Self that is defined by attributes such as curiosity, compassion, and peacefulness. distinct sections, however, might play distinct functions and impact behavior and emotions. Exiles and Protectors are the two major categories of parts.

1. Exiles are the portions that hold terrible memories, feelings, and experiences from childhood. Exiles are typically forced away from awareness because they are experiencing extreme emotions such as guilt, fear, or despair.

2. Protectors: Protectors try to protect the individual from the exiles' anguish. They might take the form of controlling, critical, or caring actions. To prevent emotions of inadequacy or guilt, a person may acquire a perfectionist personality trait.

## Managers' And Firefighters' Roles:

Managers and Firefighters are two types of Protectors.

1. Managers: These components attempt to keep control by being organized, planning ahead of time, and being in command. They frequently seem like perfectionists or overachievers.

2. Firefighters: When the exiles are stimulated and tremendous emotions occur, firefighters are activated. These portions attempt to divert the

individual's attention through impulsive activities like overeating, substance misuse, or self-harm.

## Self-Leadership Brings About Harmony:

By reaching the fundamental Self, IFS treatment seeks to promote harmony and balance among these interior aspects. The therapist helps people form relationships with their parts, assisting them in understanding the constructive intentions underlying each one and encouraging self-leadership.

## The Self-Leadership Eight Cs

The Eight Cs of Self-Leadership in Internal Family Systems indicates important core Self attributes that people aim to embody for maximum well-being and harmony within themselves. In the IFS paradigm, these Cs serve as a road map for self-discovery and healing.

1. Curiosity: Fostering curiosity entails examining many aspects of oneself with an open and nonjudgmental attitude. Curiosity helps people grasp

the motives, anxieties, and desires of their many interior components.

2. Compassion is focused on the injured and protecting components. Individuals can begin the process of healing and integration by embracing these characteristics with respect and understanding.

3. Calmness: Developing a sense of serenity is developing an internal environment in which one can stay focused and grounded even in the face of difficult emotions or events.

4. Clarity: getting clarity entails getting a thorough awareness of the responsibilities and functions of each internal component. This clarity is essential for spotting trends and making sound decisions.

5. Confidence: In the context of IFS, confidence refers to trusting one's capacity to negotiate internal difficulties. It entails cultivating self-assurance and faith in one's ability to lead and direct the internal system toward harmony.

6. Courage is required when confronting internal wounds and testing protection mechanisms. This is addressing challenging feelings and experiences with an open mind to examine and comprehend them.

7. Connectedness: Recognizing the connectivity of internal elements and cultivating a sense of oneness helps to create a more integrated and balanced internal system. Connectedness entails understanding the role of each component in the overall functioning of the individual.

8. Embracing creativity entails experimenting with new methods of responding to internal problems. It improves flexibility and enables individuals to create inventive solutions and reactions to internal tensions.

## IFS Techniques And Interventions

IFS uses several strategies and interventions to assist individuals in exploring, comprehending, and integrating their internal components. The therapy approach entails guided self-exploration, connection development with one's parts, and encouraging communication among these parts. The following are some of the most important approaches utilized in IFS therapy:

## 1. Internal Investigation:

Therapists assist individuals in exploring their internal landscape, assisting them in identifying and comprehending the many components that comprise their personality. Recognizing the duties, feelings, and memories linked with each portion is required.

## 2. Externalizing Components:

Individuals in IFS are encouraged to externalize their internal elements by naming them or seeing them as separate entities. This procedure contributes to a clearer and more concrete grasp of each component's distinct qualities.

## 3. Parts Discussion:

Therapists help individuals and their components communicate with one another. This discourse fosters compassion and empathy by allowing for a deeper understanding of the reasons and goals underlying each component.

## 4. Exiles Unburdened:

Unburdening entails assisting persons in revisiting and healing the scars held by their exiles. This may entail reliving painful experiences with the therapist's assistance, offering a possibility for reprocessing and resolution.

## 5. Re-parenting and Self-Care:

IFS emphasizes the value of self-care and re-parenting injured portions. Individuals learn to offer the care and support that was absent in their early experiences, promoting healing and self-compassion.

## 6. Conscious Awareness:

Mindfulness activities are used in IFS treatment to assist individuals in remaining present and aware of their internal experiences. Mindful awareness improves one's capacity to view and interact with internal organs without feeling overwhelmed.

**7. Bringing Polarities Together:**

IFS aims to reconcile opposites by recognizing and embracing the good intentions of both protectors and exiles. This entails striking a balance between the various sections' defensive roles and the vulnerability borne by exiles.

**8. Self-Directed Visualization:**

Individuals are led through visualization exercises that assist them in connecting with their essential Self. These visions foster self-leadership and generate a sense of safety, allowing the inner Self to take control of the internal system.

**9. Mapping of Parts:**

Visual tools, such as diagrams or drawings, are frequently used by therapists to develop a map of the internal system, highlighting the interactions between different sections. Parts mapping assists in finding trends and problem areas.

**10. Exploration of One's Future Self:**

Individuals investigate their future selves, imagining the characteristics and attributes they wish to embody. This investigation aids in the development of personal objectives and gives a road map for continued self-leadership.

Finally, Internal Family Systems therapy provides a distinct and all-encompassing approach to understanding and improving one's inner reality. Individuals can attain a better sense of self-leadership by identifying, befriending, and integrating internal components, supporting healing and personal progress. The Eight Cs of Self-Leadership gives a framework for building traits that lead to an internal system that is balanced and harmonious. IFS assists individuals on a path of self-discovery and healing using a range of approaches and interventions, establishing a deeper connection with their inner Self and supporting long-term positive transformation.

# CHAPTER THREE

## Internal Family Systems Therapy Applications

Internal Family Systems (IFS) therapy, developed by Dr. Richard Schwartz, is a therapeutic approach that views the mind as a complex system of interacting subpersonalities or "parts." These parts have distinct beliefs, emotions, and roles, and the goal of IFS therapy is to assist individuals in exploring and integrating these parts for greater harmony and self-awareness. IFS therapy's applications cover a wide spectrum of psychological disorders, making it a versatile and successful treatment choice.

1. Trauma and post-traumatic stress disorder (PTSD): IFS treatment has proven great success in treating trauma and PTSD. Trauma frequently leads to the creation of protective components that bear emotional baggage from the past. IFS assists people in connecting with these parts, understanding their functions, and working toward healing and integration.

IFS helps the unburdening of strong emotions linked with prior events by creating a caring relationship with traumatic memories.

2. Anxiety and Depression: Internal Family Systems therapy is an excellent treatment for anxiety and depression. Internal conflicts between distinct portions of the self are common with these mental health difficulties. IFS assists people in identifying and navigating these tensions, promoting a feeling of balance and self-compassion. Clients can work towards symptom relief and general well-being by understanding the underlying dynamics of anxious or depressed aspects.

3. Relationship Issues: IFS can also help with interpersonal interactions. Relationship conflicts and problems frequently reflect the interaction of several interior aspects. IFS treatment assists individuals in better understanding their relationship patterns by delving into the responsibilities of various components in the context of their interactions with others.

This self-awareness improves communication, increases empathy, and aids in the formation of healthy relationship dynamics.

4. Addiction and Substance Abuse: Addiction is frequently considered in IFS treatment as a means for some parts to cope with suffering or unfulfilled needs. Individuals can obtain insight into the underlying reasons fuelling substance usage by investigating the roles of various stages in the addiction cycle. IFS assists clients in developing a loving connection with their addicted parts, which allows for healing and the development of better coping strategies.

5. Internal Family Systems Therapy (IFST) has shown potential in the treatment of eating disorders. Exploration of body image, self-esteem, and control concerns can lead to a better understanding of the causes of disordered eating patterns. IFS supports individuals in building a more balanced and self-nurturing connection with their bodies and food by facilitating the integration of competing aspects.

6. Living with chronic disease or persistent pain frequently entails a complicated interaction of physical and emotional elements. Individuals can benefit from IFS treatment by exploring the many parts of themselves that react to pain or disease, building a deeper feeling of self-compassion and resilience. Individuals may find enhanced coping skills and a more positive attitude toward their health issues by learning and combining these components.

7. Personal Development and Self-Exploration: While Internal Family Systems Therapy is successful in treating specific mental health conditions, it is also a useful tool for personal development and self-exploration.

Individuals who are not experiencing significant psychological distress can benefit from IFS by acquiring a better grasp of their inner dynamics, increasing self-awareness, and cultivating a more integrated and authentic sense of self.

# Other Therapeutic Approaches Integration

Internal Family Systems therapy may be effectively combined with a variety of therapeutic techniques, increasing treatment efficacy and flexibility. Some of the ways IFS can supplement other modalities are as follows:

1. Cognitive-Behavioral Therapy (CBT): When IFS is combined with CBT, a holistic approach to resolving cognitive distortions and behavioral problems is achieved. CBT emphasizes modifying negative thinking patterns and actions, whereas IFS investigates the underlying emotional and mental issues that may contribute to these patterns. The combination of both techniques allows for a more comprehensive knowledge of the client's experience and fosters long-term transformation.

2. Mindfulness-Based Therapies: In its emphasis on self-awareness and nonjudgmental observation, IFS treatment is comparable to mindfulness-based therapies. Integrating mindfulness techniques with

IFS can help clients connect with their internal parts more effectively and build a thoughtful, loving relationship with themselves. To increase the examination of interior experiences, mindfulness practices may be smoothly included in IFS sessions.

3. IFS can supplement psychodynamic techniques by giving a systematic framework for understanding and working with the psyche's inherent processes. While psychodynamic therapy investigates unconscious processes and early life experiences, IFS takes a different approach by concentrating on the current interactions of various components of the self. This connection enables a more in-depth examination of the client's internal world.

4. Dialectical Behavior Therapy (DBT): Combining IFS and DBT can be effective for people who struggle with emotional dysregulation and interpersonal issues. DBT focuses on developing skills for emotion control, interpersonal effectiveness, and distress tolerance. IFS supplements these abilities by delving into the

underlying emotional conflicts and components that lead to problems with regulation and relationships.

5. Gestalt Therapy and IFS both emphasize the significance of investigating the present moment and clients' interior sensations. By combining these methodologies, a dynamic study of the client's internal and exterior world is enabled. To enable direct interactions between distinct elements of the self, Gestalt techniques such as empty chair work can be utilized in conjunction with IFS.

6. Incorporating IFS into narrative therapy improves knowledge of the tales individuals tell about themselves. IFS enables a more in-depth examination of the internal characters or pieces that contribute to these narratives. Therapists can assist clients in reconstructing more empowering and integrated life stories by combining narrative approaches with IFS.

# IFS Research And Evidence Base

Internal Family Systems treatment has seen an increase in the study, adding to the database supporting its usefulness in a variety of therapeutic settings.

1. Trauma and PTSD: Studies have demonstrated that IFS is effective in the treatment of trauma and PTSD. According to research published in the "Journal of Traumatic Stress" (2013), IFS is beneficial in lowering PTSD symptoms and enhancing general psychological well-being. The study emphasizes IFS's ability to address the intricate interaction of traumatic memories and accompanying emotional states.

2. Anxiety and depression: Several studies have shown that IFS is useful in lowering anxiety and depressive symptoms. Randomized controlled research published in the "Journal of Clinical Psychology" (2017) compared IFS to standard cognitive-behavioral treatment and discovered that both techniques were equally effective in lowering

depressive and anxiety symptoms. These data support the use of IFS as an effective treatment for mood disorders.

3. Eating Disorders: There is growing interest in using IFS to treat eating disorders. A pilot research published in the "Journal of Psychotherapy Integration" (2016) investigated the efficacy of IFS when used in combination with standard eating disorder treatment. According to the findings, IFS may have led to improvements in self-esteem, body image, and overall eating disorder symptoms.

4. Drug misuse and Addictions: While research on IFS and drug misuse is still in its early stages, the first findings are promising. A paper published in the "Journal of Addictions & Offender Counseling" (2019) explored the possible advantages of IFS in the treatment of drug use disorders by addressing the underlying emotional dynamics and internal conflicts that contribute to addictive behaviors.

5. Internal Family Systems and Neurobiology: Neurobiological research is also being conducted to investigate the influence of IFS on the brain. Neuroimaging was employed in a research published in "Frontiers in Psychology" (2020) to investigate the brain alterations related to IFS. According to the findings, IFS therapies were linked to favorable improvements in brain activity related to emotional control and self-awareness.

6. Personal Development and Well-Being: Research on the use of IFS for personal development and well-being is underway. IFS has been shown in studies to promote self-awareness, self-compassion, and general psychological well-being in people who do not have particular clinical conditions. This lends credence to the notion that IFS is not just a pathological therapy but also a helpful instrument for personal growth.

Finally, Internal Family Systems treatment is beneficial in treating a wide range of psychological conditions, from trauma and PTSD to anxiety, depression, and relationship problems. Because of its integrative character, it may be seamlessly integrated with different treatment modalities, increasing its adaptability. An increasing corpus of research offers empirical support for IFS's efficacy in a variety of clinical applications, adding to its acceptance as a viable treatment modality. Internal Family Systems therapy is anticipated to play an increasingly major position in the field of psychotherapy as research advances, providing clients with a unique and transforming path to healing and self-discovery.

# CHAPTER FOUR

## Internal Family Systems Therapy: Issues And Criticism

Dr. Richard Schwartz's Internal Family Systems (IFS) treatment has received acclaim for its novel approach to understanding and treating the human psyche. However, IFS, like every therapy approach, has its obstacles and critics. It is essential to investigate these factors to acquire a complete picture of the therapy and its possible limits.

One problem with IFS is the possibility of client opposition. Parts—distinct components of the self that may convey emotions, memories, or beliefs—can be difficult for some people to understand at first. Clients may find it difficult to understand that different portions of themselves may have opposing feelings or views. Furthermore, for clients who are not used to exploring their inner world in such an organized fashion, the process of recognizing and connecting with these sections may be scary.

Another criticism leveled about IFS is its focus on self-therapy. While the treatment encourages individuals to autonomously study and comprehend their systems, detractors say that this method may not be appropriate for everyone. Some clients may prefer a more directed approach to treatment, with the therapist playing a more active role in directing the process. Certain people may find the degree of introspection necessary in IFS to be too much for them, and they may benefit from a more supporting and guided therapy approach.

Furthermore, IFS has drawn criticism for seeing parts as separate things. Some critics contend that this internal diversity oversimplifies the intricacies of human awareness. IFS metaphorical terminology, such as "exiles," "managers," and "firefighters," has been challenged for lacking factual foundation and perhaps encouraging a reductionist view of the human mind.

Furthermore, some therapists may find it difficult to effectively integrate IFS into their established therapeutic frameworks. Adopting IFS can be a steep learning curve, and therapists may struggle to use its concepts successfully in their practice. This problem underlines the significance of thorough training and regular supervision for therapists who want to implement IFS into their practice.

Despite these obstacles, many practitioners and clients attest to IFS's transforming power. It is critical to understand that the critiques and obstacles do not contradict the therapy's efficacy, but rather indicate areas that may require additional refining and customization to fit the unique requirements of clients.

## Internal Family Systems Training And Certification

Internal Family Systems (IFS) treatment involves extensive training and certification to guarantee that therapists have the essential abilities and grasp of the paradigm. IFS training is intended to provide therapists with the tools they need to help clients through the examination of their internal systems and support recovery. Let's look at the most important parts of IFS training and certification.

Completing the Level 1 Training is the first step toward becoming an IFS therapist. Participants will learn about the existence of parts, the notion of Self, and the therapeutic process of accessing and balancing the internal system.

It covers the theoretical background as well as the practical skills required to implement IFS concepts in a therapeutic environment.

After completing Level 1 training, therapists can progress to Level 2 and Level 3 training. These advanced courses go further into the complexities of IFS therapy, including subjects like coping with trauma, addressing systemic issues, and honing therapeutic abilities. Advanced training enables therapists to have a more sophisticated grasp of the model and how it may be applied to a wide range of clinical difficulties.

The training process is incomplete without supervision and consultation. Therapists get instruction and comments from experienced IFS practitioners during supervision. This real-time assistance assists therapists in navigating challenging situations, honing their abilities, and expanding their grasp of the model.

Ongoing consultation ensures that therapists continue to effectively integrate IFS into their practice while also addressing any problems that may occur.

To obtain IFS certification, therapists must complete all levels of training, accrue a certain number of hours of direct IFS therapy, and be supervised. Certification acknowledges a therapist's expertise in applying IFS principles and their commitment to upholding a high quality of practice. It assures customers that the therapist has undertaken extensive training and meets key criteria to properly offer IFS treatment.

In the IFS community, continuing education is promoted, with chances for therapists to attend workshops, conferences, and specialized training to improve their abilities and keep current on advances in the area. This dedication to continuous learning means that therapists are well-equipped to meet a wide range of client requirements and issues.

Dr. Richard Schwartz developed the IFS Institute, which oversees the training and certification procedure. The institution provides a structured curriculum, workshops, and conferences, as well as tools for therapists looking to further their knowledge of IFS. The global network of IFS-trained therapists creates a community of practitioners who can share thoughts, cooperate, and contribute to the model's continued progress.

## Internal Family Systems Therapy In The Future

Internal Family Systems (IFS) treatment is changing, and numerous intriguing future paths are emerging as the profession gains recognition and acceptance.

These advancements represent the treatment model's continual improvement as well as its adaption to handle a larger spectrum of clinical concerns. Let's look at some of the important factors influencing the future of IFS treatment.

Integration of IFS with other therapy methods is one potential avenue. While IFS is a full paradigm in and of itself, therapists are experimenting with combining it with treatments such as mindfulness-based therapies, somatic experience, and dialectical behavior therapy. Integrating IFS with other evidence-based techniques can improve its efficacy and expand its application to a wider range of clinical groups.

Another area of development is the application of IFS to specific demographics and circumstances. Therapists are investigating how IFS might be adjusted to meet the specific requirements of those suffering from complicated trauma, eating disorders, and chronic medical issues. IFS effectiveness is being studied in a variety of settings, including schools, organizations, and community mental health initiatives.

Technological advancements are also shaping the future of IFS treatment. Individuals can now get IFS therapy remotely because of the proliferation of online platforms and healthcare providers. This move brings up new opportunities for engaging marginalized communities, removing geographical boundaries, and giving customers with flexible alternatives.

The study of the neurological basis of IFS is gaining traction. As neuroscience progresses, there is a rising interest in understanding how IFS therapies affect the brain and contribute to favorable therapeutic results. The neuroscientific study might give empirical support for the pathways that facilitate healing and change in IFS.

IFS's continuing global development encourages cross-cultural partnerships and adaptations. Therapists from many cultural origins are implementing IFS ideas into their practice, helping to cross-pollinate therapeutic techniques. This cross-cultural communication benefits the IFS community by promoting a more comprehensive knowledge of the human psyche.

The IFS community is also dedicated to tackling issues of social justice and creating equity in the profession. Efforts are being made to make IFS training and materials available to a wide spectrum of therapists and clients. An essential part of IFS's future growth will be the investigation of how it might assist in the healing of collective trauma and systematic oppression.

As IFS develops, constant discourse and collaboration among therapists, researchers, and the larger mental health community will be critical in guiding its course. The emphasis on humility, curiosity, and openness to new ideas guarantees that the IFS model stays dynamic and sensitive to the changing environment of mental health treatment. The future of IFS promises more innovation, more accessibility, and a better understanding of the complex workings of the human mind and spirit.

## Conclusion

Finally, Internal Family Systems (IFS) treatment provides a transformational and integrative approach to psychotherapy that acknowledges the human mind's plurality. IFS, developed by Richard Schwartz, holds that people have several inner "parts" or sub-personalities that impact their ideas, feelings, and behaviors. The treatment seeks to bring these aspects into harmony, resulting in a more balanced and honest sense of self.

Clients learn to comprehend, speak with, and eventually integrate these internal elements via the process of inquiry and discourse. This integration increases self-awareness, emotional control, and decision-making ability. Acknowledging and resolving defensive aspects that may have emerged in reaction to prior trauma allows individuals to reach their inner, loving Self.

The IFS emphasis on the Self as a calm, loving, and confident core promotes resilience and self-healing. Individuals are encouraged to adopt a thoughtful and inquiring attitude toward their interior sensations as part of the therapy. Clients may then manage life's obstacles with more comfort and sincerity.

Internal Family Systems stands out in the field of psychotherapy for its empowering and non-pathologizing approach. IFS provides a viable route for personal growth, healing, and the development of a more integrated and harmonious self by acknowledging and valuing the complexity of the human mind.

# THE END